Training Social Services Staff: Evidence from new research
Research in Social Work Education no.4

Published 1996
by the National Institute for Social Work
5 Tavistock Place, London WC1H 9SN

ISBN 1 899942 12 2

TRAINING SOCIAL SERVICES STAFF:

EVIDENCE FROM NEW RESEARCH

Report of a conference organised by
the National Institute for Social Work and
the Universities of Edinburgh and Sheffield

24 April 1996

Edited by Naomi Connelly

November 1996

RESEARCH IN SOCIAL WORK EDUCATION No.4

TRAINING SOCIAL SERVICES STAFF: EVIDENCE FROM NEW RESEARCH

Contents

INTRODUCTION

Naomi Connelly

This report provides a record of a conference on 'Training Social Services Staff: Evidence from New Research'. The conference was organised by Susan Balloch, National Institute for Social Work (NISW), in association with Peter Marsh, University of Sheffield. The Central Council for Education and Training in Social Work subsidised the conference through a generous grant. The event was held at NISW in London, and was chaired by NISW's Director, Daphne Statham.

The conference focused on two important pieces of research funded by the Department of Health. The first concerns the 'readiness to practise' of newly qualified social workers. The research was carried out by the Universities of Sheffield and Edinburgh, and the paper by Peter Marsh and John Triseliotis which opens this report presents information about the study and summarises its findings.

The second piece of research is an ongoing survey of the social services workforce. This is being conducted by the NISW Research Unit. Susan Balloch describes the wide-ranging study, and she and Jay Ginn set out some of the findings relating to education and training.

The remainder of the report provides material from the five workshops, covering a great range of subjects and issues, which formed part of the conference day. Some accounts take the form of a paper written by the person who introduced the workshop, while others have been put together from overheads, summaries and notes on the day.

We are very grateful to all those who shared their information, ideas and experience and made the day such a thought-provoking occasion. Many important questions were raised. Some of these reflected longstanding concerns but others seemed very much a product of changing ideas, structures and contexts in the late 1990s. All were illustrative of the continuing attempt to find a better fit between the education and training of those working in social services and the challenges of their task.

Many thanks are also due to Rose Freeman who masterminded the arrangements and ensured the smooth running of the conference.

SOCIAL WORKERS: THEIR TRAINING AND FIRST YEAR IN WORK

Peter Marsh
Senior Lecturer, Department of Sociological Studies, University of Sheffield

John Triseliotis
Professor, Department of Social Policy and Social Work, University of Edinburgh

Between 1987 and 1990 Sheffield and Edinburgh Universities, with financial support and encouragement from the Central Council for Education and Training in Social Work (CCETSW), the Economic and Social Research Council and the Joseph Rowntree Foundation, ran three workshops which focused on outcomes in social work education. The aim of the workshops was to develop a research strategy for social work education, an aim which grew from widespread concern that there was a paucity of research in social work education. This was proving detrimental at a time of rapid changes and when so much of the criticism for failure in social work practice was levelled at training. The lack of any form of research strategy seemed a serious and pressing matter.

Consequently, the first two workshops concentrated on what needed to be researched. The focus of the third was on how the research questions could be addressed. The papers have now been published (Marsh and Clark, 1990). One of the main research priorities identified by the workshops was that of 'training for competent practice'.

The theme of practice competency in social work is a broad and complex one which can (and should) be studied in a number of different ways.

One such way was the study undertaken by the same two universities and described here. It was funded by the Department of Health and the Scottish Office, and was designed to form part of the baseline for the research strategy outlined in the earlier seminars. Its main focus was the match or mismatch between course output and agency expectations in the first year of practice. After examining student evaluations of their training, the study moved on to provide a detailed review of the practice reality facing staff in their first year. It looked at their perceived ability to handle this first year, and the support available in policy and in action. It also examined the agency response to apparent gaps in ability, particularly as represented by the arrangements for training and support in this first year.

Competent practice

Detailed definitions of competent social work practice remain the subject of debate. As a result, usable criteria against which performance can be measured are few. Even if there were clear agreement, it is still important to examine the early practice years along with the courses. For example, it may be that newly qualified staff are expected to be competent in high risk areas very soon after qualification. (In CCETSW's 1988 study of areas of work undertaken immediately after courses, and one year on, 13 per cent of newly appointed staff and 22 per cent of staff after one year said that 'child abuse/children at risk' was the major client group with which they worked.) The initial period of practice will always be a testing one, and this study paid due attention to the general difficulties faced by all new professionals. Empirical knowledge concerning agency expectations of newly qualified staff is an important context for judgements concerning training outcome.

It must also be equally clear that preparing students to help people resolve social problems successfully requires, among other things, that training fits well with the kind of (appropriate) tasks allocated to staff after qualification, and that training provides the knowledge, skills and attitudes which staff require. This study examined the apparent gaps in knowledge, skills and attitudes via the perceptions of staff and the requirements of agency policy and procedure.

Although only a few studies have been undertaken so far, these indicate that the relationship between the academic content of training and social work practice is problematic. Stevenson and Parsloe's 1978 study of practitioner views considered 'some educational implications' and perhaps paved the way for the research reported here. Small scale studies by Carew (1979), Corby (1982), Gibbs and Cigno (1986), Pilalis (1986) and Waterhouse (1987) indicate that social workers make little use of the theoretical material taught on courses in their subsequent practice. The accounts in our study support this view, and also start to explain some of the fundamental problems that underlie it.

Davies' and his colleagues' studies of training for social services and probation (Davies, 1984; Davies and Wright, 1989; Boswell et al, 1993) start to develop an empirical view on the link between courses and practice. The present study, because of depth, scale and focus, is able to take this work further. A number of other studies have looked at some other aspects of the educational process, but no other study to our knowledge has examined in any detail what happens to the newly qualified during their first year in employment. The crucial transition period from training to work, when the results of training may be at their most visible, has been effectively unresearched.

The study
The research strategy was developed on the relative strengths and limitations of existing designs, selected following an extensive literature review (Secker and Clark, 1990). The study was therefore descriptive and analytic in approach, developing its ideas from the data presented in order to construct theory relevant to the understanding of the 'fit' between all the key elements of social work education and training and the first year of practice.

The study began soon after the introduction of the gradual replacement of the Certificate of Qualification in Social Work (CQSW) with the Diploma in Social Work (DipSW) qualification. As one of the aims of the study was to explore the impact of the change from CQSW to DipSW, it was important to make sure that the effects of newness (of DipSW) and of running down (of CQSW) were minimised. Research judgements had not been used to build the new qualification—the research had not been there to use. Many of the conceptual issues were sidestepped by a continued campaign to persuade government to agree to the extension of training from two to three years. An alternative view was that the quality of induction and in-service training programmes (including supervision) provided to newly qualified staff might be a more decisive factor in consolidating and enhancing competence to practise than the extension of training.

The findings of the present study contribute to a firmer base for the continuing development of social work training. The study identified some of the key areas for attention and evaluated one of the hallmarks of the new qualification - the development of closer collaborative arrangements between education and practice agencies. This process was designed to establish a better connection between theory and practice on the course and a closer fit between course output and the requirements of the job. It was meant to improve 'readiness to practise'. For the researchers it was also a unique opportunity to test this significant and expensive (Gray and Cox, 1991) development at the time of changeover of qualification when old and new could be compared.

The aims of the study
The research set out to establish how prepared to practise newly qualified social workers and probation officers were during their first year of employment. It was centrally concerned with the 'fit' between training and employment, exploring course content and outcome, and how staff were deployed, given in-service training and supported. Prominence was given to the views of the newly qualified staff themselves, but an important check on their views was given by asking seniors/supervisors of newly qualified staff how they estimated the skills, expertise and overall 'fit' of their new staff.

The views presented in the study suggest many questions which could and should be contrasted and compared with those of course staff. A study of course staff logically follows this one, and it is to be hoped that their views, in the light of this research, will be sought in due course.

The research was designed to:

- provide a detailed overall description of the education and training provided on courses and in agencies in the first year of practice
- establish the perceptions of newly qualified social workers about the effectiveness of their training in relation to the development of particular knowledge, skills, aptitudes and values deemed important for practice
- monitor retrospectively the first year induction period, and deployment in practice, of the newly qualified social workers
- identify the tasks delegated to them and the match between these tasks and their earlier training (with especial reference to developments in child care and community care)
- establish the nature of supervision made available and its relevance to clients' needs and newly qualified staff's own needs

- examine the perception of knowledge, skills and abilities required for a selection of the tasks allocated, as seen through the eyes of the first line managers
- contrast levels of perceived readiness to practise in relation to different groups of courses, especially DipSW and CQSW approaches to training
- provide some additional insights concerning differences and similarities between English and Scottish social work education.

At an early stage, the decision was taken to include the probation service in the study. A substantial group of staff was involved, and in comparing and contrasting them with social workers it was thought that there might be important lessons about 'readiness'. This has turned out to be the case.

Research design

A longitudinal approach was adopted in order to obtain views shortly after qualifying and views based on some nine months of practice. This allowed the newly qualified staff to reflect on their course when it was fresh in their minds, and also to do so with the benefit of hindsight and the day-to-day experience of the needs of practice. It also allowed them to comment about expectations of practice, and the reality they faced. One-off views were likely to be reduced with this approach and questions could be put slightly differently at the two stages in order to gain maximum insight into problems and issues.

Using questionnaires, data was gathered from a sample of 714 social workers and probation officers who qualified from CQSW and DipSW courses in 1992 and 1993, shortly after they had completed their course and then around nine months later when they were in practice. In addition, using a semi-structured schedule, interviews were carried out with 60 of the 1993 DipSW newly qualified staff. Sixty-nine supervisors of newly qualified staff (seniors) answered a questionnaire on their views of the newly qualified, and 31 interviews were carried out, again using a semi-structured schedule. Plans to interview a representative sample of clients of newly qualified staff had to be abandoned. The overall design of the study is summarised in the following diagram.

Figure 1: Overall design of the study

1992
Newly qualified

| End of course Questionnaire |
| 1st Year of work Questionnaire |

1993 Newly qualified

| End of course Questionnaire | |
| 1st Year of work Questionnaire | Interviews |

Supervisors/Seniors

| Supervisors' Questionnaire | Interviews |

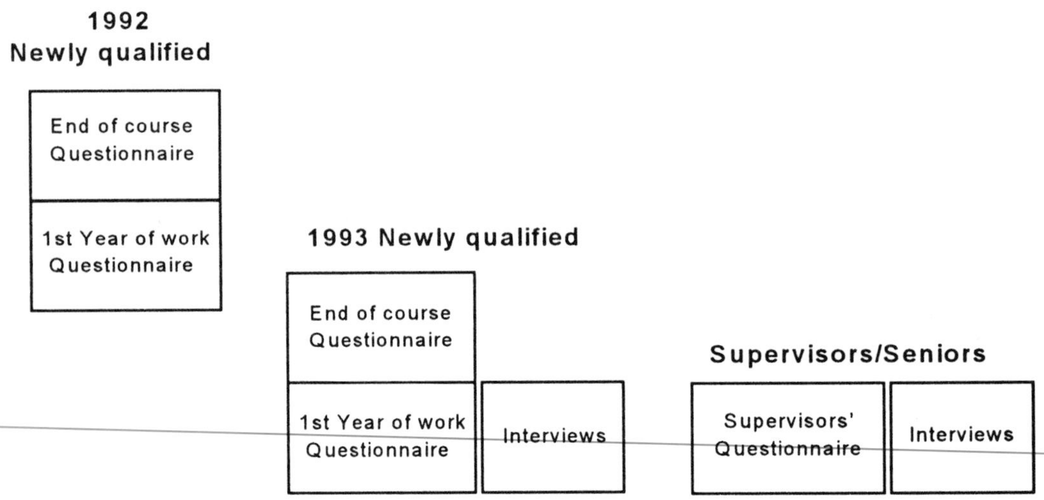

Some general findings

The detailed findings of the study have been published (Marsh and Triseliotis, 1996) and summary of findings is also available from the authors. The overall picture to emerge about social work training is an encouraging one, but some important problems still remain. Many able and highly competent people come into social work through training and significant improvements have taken place over the last 15 or so years, but better outcomes could still be achieved with greater attention paid to the main drawbacks identified by the study. However, significant congruence between expected competencies and the DipSW qualification was especially found in relation to probation training, suggesting that congruence is an achievable objective to aim for, and that key elements of probation training should be developed as the general mode of social work education.

Many of the problems faced by training are related to the diverse expectations of that training, including the lack of consensus regarding breadth and depth, and regarding genericism and specialism. Insufficient attention paid to key subject areas within particular specialisms, for example work with children and families, is a key finding of the study.

Being knowledgeable about applied research and theory, learning about this research and theory in practical ways, and having practice teachers and supervisors who were well versed in this area was identified by the study as very important. Newly qualified social workers use and value theory in their practice and a significant percentage want more of it, but it is clear that it needs to be better taught and understood, both on courses and in the first year of practice.

While practice opportunities and practice teaching were found to be a key element of training, the study also identified some very poor practices which could all too easily be overlooked but which require some urgent attention. Although it was clear that there had been substantial improvements in practice-teaching it was still the case that a sizeable minority of students experienced at least one poor placement. It also became clear that the development of practice-teacher accreditation, and of a practice-teaching specialism which was completely separate from first year supervision and from practice tutors on courses could, if carried too far, contribute to the very problems that it was designed to resolve.

Many newly qualified staff started work with uncertainties and apprehensions. After a year most of them valued their qualification, but many also perceived what they and the seniors described as the increased bureaucratisation of social work. This was viewed as largely alien both to the motives and values that brought them into social work and to much of their recent training. The serious tensions found between the expectations of newly qualified staff (and possibly of their trainers) and those of employers need addressing.

Employers or their representatives have often criticised social work courses - sometimes rightly - for not preparing students for the realities of practice. With the exception of the probation service, many agencies could equally be criticised for largely failing the newly qualified in their first year in work: the quality of induction and supervision came under sustained criticism. Even in-service training was rarely tailored to the specific needs of the newly qualified and was all too often not available at the right time.

The evidence from the research data highlights the importance of planning for a continuum between training and the first year in work. These two are largely indivisible and cannot be considered or understood as two separate entities. To talk about an extension to training without recognising and taking account of this reality is to view training in over-linear terms and without considering the interplay between courses and the first year that is the foundation of readiness.

In conclusion, trainers and CCETSW can take credit for many of the improvements that have taken place in education and training over the last ten or so years. With one or two exceptions, the encouraging results appear to have been the outcome of gradual change rather than being a sole artefact of the new qualification. Some of the serious drawbacks identified in this study need discussion and action. In this respect the study provides a challenge for trainers, employers, CCETSW and the government.

Acknowledgements and disclaimer
We are very grateful for the work of Joan Hanson as Senior Research Fellow on the study, and for the time and effort of all of the students and staff who participated.

The study was funded by the Department of Health and the Scottish Office but the views expressed here are those of the authors and not necessarily those of the Department of Health or the Scottish Office.

References
Boswell, G., Davies, M. and Wright, A. (1993) *Contemporary Probation Practice*, Avebury, Aldershot.
Carew, R. (1979) 'The place of knowledge in social work activity', *British Journal of Social Work* 9,3: 349-364.
Corby, B. (1982) 'Theory and practice in long term social work', *British Journal of Social Work* 12,6: 619-663.
Davies, M. (1984) 'Training: what we think of it now', *Social Work Today*, 24 January, pp.12-17.
Davies, M. and Wright, A. (1989), *Probation Training: A consumer perspective*, HMSO, London.
Gibbs, I. and Cigno, K. (1986) 'Reflections from the field: the experience of former CSS and CQSW students', *British Journal of Social Work* 16,3: 289-309.
Gray, J. and Cox, R. (1991) *A Study of the Implementation of Regulations and Requirements*, Centre for Higher Education Studies, University of London, London.
Marsh, P. and Clark, C. (eds) (1990) 'Research issues in social work education and training', *Research in Social Work Education* No.1, Universities of Sheffield and Edinburgh, Sheffield.
Marsh, P. and Triseliotis, J. (1996), *Ready to Practise? Social workers and probation officers: their training and first year in work*, Avebury, Aldershot.

Pilalis, J. (1986) 'The integration of theory and practice: a re-examination of a paradoxical expectation', *British Journal of Social Work* 16,1: 79-96.

Secker, J. and Clark, C. (1990), *A Bibliography of Relevant Research in Social Work Education and Training*, Universities of Edinburgh and Sheffield, Edinburgh.

Stevenson, O. and Parsloe, P. (1978) *Social Service Teams: The practitioner's view*, HMSO, London.

Waterhouse, L. (1987) 'The relationship between theory and practice in social work training', *Issues in Social Work Education* 7,1: 3-19.

EXPERIENCES OF TRAINING IN THE STATUTORY SOCIAL SERVICES

Susan Balloch
Senior Researcher, National Institute for Social Work

The National Institute for Social Work (NISW) panel survey of the social services workforce was set up in 1992 with funding from the Department of Health. It has three main objectives:
- to describe and understand the dynamics of the statutory workforce, in terms of the stability, mobility and attrition of staff
- to evaluate the experiences of the workforce, in particular their levels of satisfaction and dissatisfaction, their experiences of physical violence, threatening or abusive behaviour and racism, and their levels of stress
- to assess the uptake and impact of training and of new qualifications such as National Vocational Qualifications (NVQs) and the Diploma in Social Work(DipSW).

Following preparation for the survey in five social services departments in England, similar surveys were instigated in two social work districts in Scotland and in the four Boards and related Trusts in Northern Ireland.

This paper and the following one by Jay Ginn use data from the first wave of the survey in England and focus on some of the findings related to education and training. (See Balloch et al. 1995 and Ginn et al. forthcoming.) The second wave of interviews was completed in the last three months of 1995 and findings from these interviews will become available in 1997.

Methodology
During 1993 a random sample was drawn of managers, social workers, home care workers and residential workers in the social services departments of five local authorities. These authorities included a rural county, an inner and an outer London borough, and two metropolitan districts in different parts of the country. These authorities were included not just because of their geographical and organisational spread but also because they held personnel lists which were more or less computerised. In spite of this, the researchers found a 12 per cent inaccuracy in the personnel data from which the sample was drawn. The five local authorities were not representative of all English local authorities. However, the many striking similarities between them, which emerged as the analysis of the workforce data proceeded, make it reasonable to generalise from them to other local authorities.

The four job types mentioned above are broad employment categories. Managers include central, strategic managers below Director level, team leaders, officers in charge of residential homes and home care organisers. Social workers include field social workers and social work assistants. Home care staff are the most homogeneous category, including domiciliary staff delivering domestic and personal care to individuals in their own homes. Residential staff include staff working in all types of residential homes, from care assistants to assistant officers in charge. Some staff were deliberately excluded in order to narrow the sample to manageable proportions; these included day centre staff and occupational therapists. When drawing the sample, provision was made to over sample black staff and men. Black staff were those who defined themselves as 'other than white'.

The sample was interviewed by Social and Community Planning Research (SCPR) between October 1993 and March 1994. A fully structured questionnaire was used. This included a main questionnaire, a short self completion questionnaire and a work history questionnaire which traced the individual's employment history from the first job held in social care. In all, 1276 staff were interviewed. Because of over sampling black staff and men, the numbers were weighted for analysis in order to reflect the original population, giving a weighted total of 933 staff. Percentages quoted in the following tables are based on this weighted data.

Background findings

In the sample, 12 per cent were managers, 15 per cent social workers, 42 per cent home care workers and 31 per cent residential workers, emphasising that the majority of social services staff are engaged in domiciliary or residential work. Eighty six per cent were women and 15 per cent were black. There was some variation in the gender distribution between authorities, with the staff of one metropolitan district being made up of over 90 per cent of women. A higher percentage of men worked in the inner London borough.

Figure 1 shows the differences between women and men in the whole sample and within each job type. The over representation of men in management is as noticeable as is their under representation in home care work.

Figure 1
Gender composition of the workforce: percentages in each job type

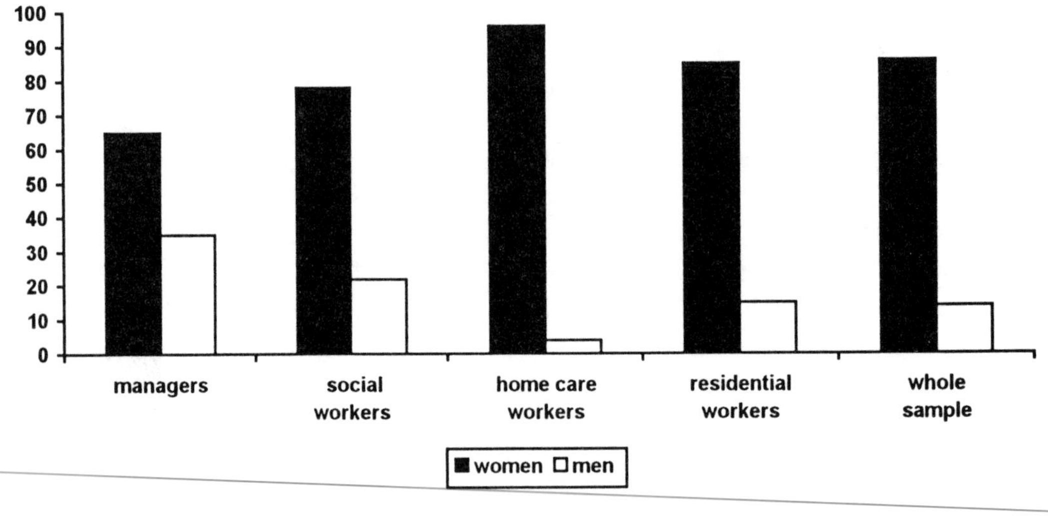

Table 1 shows the differences in the employment of black and white staff in the whole sample and within each job type. Black staff were found to be over represented in residential work and, to a lesser extent, in social work, but under represented in management and home care work.

Table 1
Ethnic composition of the workforce: percentages by job type

Job type	Whole sample	White staff	Black staff
Managers	12	12	8
Social workers	15	14	21
Home care workers	42	45	26
Residential workers	31	28	45

Figure 2 shows the differences between women and men who work full or part time. Part time working is becoming of increasing importance in the labour force and is known to be associated with low pay, reduced career prospects, limited access to training and temporary status. In the panel, in all job types, women were more likely to work part time than men. The gender differences in English social services departments may be greater than shown in our sample because one of the five authorities in the sample has a policy of only employing full time staff. If percentages were based on the other four authorities, the differences between men and women would be greater than illustrated. In social work, for example, a quarter of women would then be shown to be working part time. Clearly, in home care work, a large majority of women work part time.

Figure 2
Percentages employed full time, by gender and job type

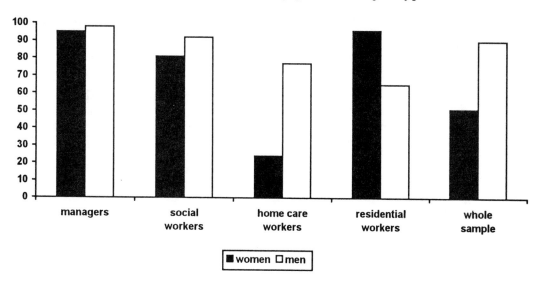

The social services workforce is relatively mature, as illustrated in Table 2. Less than ten per cent of the workforce is aged below thirty except for those working in residential care. While the majority of the workforce is aged between 30 and 49, over 40 per cent of home care staff are aged 50 or over. Women working in management, social work or residential care tend to be older than men, with a higher proportion aged 50 or over. Research has shown that older workers, and particularly women, tend to be excluded from training programmes, so this is another aspect of the social services workforce which training managers need to take into account.

Table 2
Age structure of the workforce: percentages of women and men in each job type

Age	Managers		Social workers		Home care workers		Residential workers	
	women	men	women	men	women	men	women	men
under 30	0	5	9	6	6	10	17	29
30-39	29	36	31	51	18	22	17	38
40-49	45	48	39	32	36	8	32	20
50+	26	12	21	11	40	49	34	13

Education and qualifications

Table 3 shows the highest educational qualification achieved by each job type. While for over a third of managers and social workers a degree is the highest qualification, few home care or residential staff are likely to have obtained anything higher than an 'O' level or GCSE. For those who failed to respond to the question from which this information was taken, it is reasonable to assume that no qualifications have been obtained. This leaves nearly two thirds of home care staff and half of residential staff without any educational qualifications at all. This is the base line from which social services training has to proceed.

Table 3
Highest educational qualification: percentages by job type

Qualification	Managers	Social workers	Home care workers	Residential workers
Degree (first or higher)	36	37	1	5
HND/HNC	7	9	1	1
A levels	15	22	5	6
O levels/ GCSE	21	17	17	22
Others	13	8	15	19
No response	9	8	61	48

Analysing the percentage of staff holding any type of professional qualification for social care (excluding health care) and, more narrowly, the percentage of staff holding a CQSW or its equivalent (DipSW, CSS or Home Office letter of accreditation), was a difficult exercise. The range of qualifications was substantial and the researchers remain dissatisfied with the accuracy of the percentages shown in Table 4. Questions on these issues have therefore been rephrased and asked again in the second wave of interviews which took place at the end of 1995. Results will be reported in the final research report in 1997. Meanwhile, it seems that about half of managers, three quarters of social workers, less than ten per cent of residential staff and less than one per cent of home care staff hold a CQSW or its equivalent.

Although the detailed comparison of the five authorities cannot be shown here, their results indicated that over 90 per cent of social workers held a social work qualification in one authority compared with less than 70 per cent in another. Variation between authorities may partly depend on the age composition of the workforce, with older staff less likely to be qualified, but further analysis is needed to verify this.

Table 4
Professional qualifications in social care: percentages by job type

Job type	CQSW or equivalent	Any professional qualification (including CQSW or equivalent)
Managers	54	66
Social workers	76	83
Social work assistants	3	23
Home care workers	<1	7
Residential workers	8	25

Training in the current job
Tables 5 to 10 illustrate some interesting findings on the panel's experience of training. Less than half had received any form of introductory training for the job they were holding at the time of their first interview, including less than a third of managers. Of those who had received such training, a third or more judged it to have been insufficient (Table 5).

Table 5
Introductory training for current job: percentages by job type

Job type	Received introductory training	Training judged insufficient
Managers	32	44
Social workers	47	33
Home care workers	47	34
Residential workers	40	40

Departments were well provided with information on training, but managers were the only employees likely to receive a personal list of available courses (Table 6). Home care staff fared less well from general departmental provision, and only about a quarter received personal information. As most home care staff lack both educational and professional qualifications, there are good grounds for a review of the training information policy affecting them. Less than one fifth of residential workers received personal information, although most said they were provided with a general list in their workplace. Again, raising the level of qualifications among residential workers could be supported by providing better personal information on training opportunities.

Table 6
Information on training provided by social services departments:
percentages by job type

Job type	Received general list of training courses	Received personal copy of list
Managers	97	62
Social workers	92	23
Home care workers	60	27
Residential workers	88	17

There was impressive evidence of the amount of work-related studying and training being undertaken by staff in the year before their interview. In the whole sample, 16 per cent had been studying for a qualification and 61 per cent had taken one or more short, non-qualifying courses (Table 7). Roughly between a fifth and a quarter of managers, social workers and residential workers had been studying for a qualification, but only eight per cent of home care workers. Almost all managers and social workers had taken at least one in-service course, as had nearly two thirds of residential workers and 40 per cent of home care workers.

Table 7
Training taken in twelve months prior to interview: percentages by job type

Job type	Training for work-related qualifications	In-service training not related to qualifications
Managers	27	93
Social workers	23	90
Home care workers	8	40
Residential workers	20	62
Whole sample	16	61

The career expectations of those studying for a qualification were analysed and contrasted with those who were not studying (Table 8). Managers and social workers in this group were significantly more likely to expect to have moved on to another job or to have been promoted within the two years following their interview, than were

14

their colleagues who were not studying. The reverse, however, was true for residential workers, with a majority of those studying for a qualification expecting to be in the same job in two years time. This suggests that a main reason for studying for a qualification for managers and social workers may be career mobility, whereas for residential workers the focus is on improving current job performance. Perhaps this may also mean that gaining a qualification while in residential work stabilises the individual, a factor of some importance in a group characterised by a high turnover of staff.

Table 8
Aspirations of staff training for a qualification compared with those
not doing so: percentages by job type

Aspirations	Managers		Social workers		Residential workers	
	training for qual.	not doing so	training for qual.	not doing so	training for qual.	not doing so
Expect to be in same job in two years' time	28	34	31	50	49	56
Expect to have moved on to another job or been promoted	60	47	57	36	34	30
Expect to be doing something else	12	16	13	8	13	13

Short, non-qualifying courses met with substantial approval from staff. Eighty nine per cent of the panel thought such courses helped them to do their job better, 81 per cent thought they gained new skills, 79 per cent reported improved confidence, 58 per cent gained a new network of contacts and 56 per cent improved their understanding of equal opportunities. Such courses were seen by only 44 per cent to be related to career prospects.

Whether studying for qualifications, or undertaking in-service training, managers and social workers received little departmental support (Table 9). Eighty seven per cent of managers and 84 per cent of social workers had their workload left for them to do later and there was little help by way of a reduced workload, cover from a colleague, or cover from additional staff. In comparison, home care workers and residential workers did receive cover from a colleague, though workloads were not normally reduced and additional staff were only brought in for a quarter of residential workers. Even in this group of staff, whose front line services are indispensable for their clients, over a quarter had their work left to do later. This shows that considerable difficulties and stresses must affect both those undertaking training and their colleagues who are called upon to cover for them.

Table 9
Workload cover while studying: percentages by job type

Workload cover	Managers	Social workers	Home care workers	Residential workers
Reduced while studying	5	29	43	25
Covered by colleague	35	21	76	85
Covered by additional staff	5	8	5	28
Left to do later	87	84	28	28

Note: Percentages do not add up to 100 because more than one option can apply.

Notwithstanding this, as shown in Table 10, the level of interest in training, both for qualifications and in-service, short courses, is very high among social services staff. Interest in the two types of training is fairly evenly divided within each job type, though there is a clear preference on the part of residential workers for qualifying training, and among social workers, most of whom already have a qualification, for in-service training. There are therefore grounds for considerable optimism for the future training of social services staff, as long as adequate supports are put in place.

Table 10
Interest in training: percentages by job type

Interest in training	Whole sample	Managers	Social workers	Home care workers	Residential workers
Not very interested	12	2	2	17	15
Interested in training but not in quals.	41	52	56	41	29
Interested in training for better quals.	46	44	40	42	56

Black staff

Black staff were similar to white staff in their experiences of education and training. They were significantly more likely, however, to hold a named educational qualification and black social workers were more likely than white social workers to hold a CQSW or equivalent qualification. Black staff were much more interested in training for qualifications than in taking short courses, 71 per cent compared with 29 per cent, whereas white staff were evenly divided in their interest in the two types of training. In the light of the previous discussion, it could be surmised that black staff are

16

more concerned about making progress in their career than white staff, but this would need to be qualified by further research.

Conclusion

We have presented some of the most striking findings relevant to training in the social services from the panel survey's first wave of interviews. The second wave of interviews was completed in December 1995, on average about two years after the first interviews. SCPR re-interviewed 940 staff who were still working in their original social services departments. The remaining 336 staff have also been followed up by the NISW researchers and about 100 have so far been interviewed by telephone. Of the remainder, many are known to have retired or left social services for other work. Our second report, in 1997, will analyse their movements. It will also consider the training experiences of the various groups of staff between their two interviews and the relationship of these to their mobility and their work experiences. Of particular interest in this context will be the take up of the new qualifications. A final report, in 1997, will draw together all our findings and their policy implications.

References

Balloch, S., Andrew, T., Ginn, J., McLean, J., Pahl, J. and Williams, J. (1995) *Working in the Social Services*, National Institute for Social Work, London.

Ginn, J., Andrew, T., McLean, J. and Balloch, S. (1997) *Working in the Social Services: An analysis of work histories*, National Institute for Social Work, London.

GENDER, CAREER PROGRESS AND QUALIFICATIONS

Jay Ginn
Researcher, National Institute for Social Work

In social services, as in other public sector institutions, women predominate numerically yet are under-represented in senior positions. The research on which this paper is based was designed to investigate how seniority is related to work history but measures of qualifications were included in the analysis. The data are drawn from the NISW panel survey of the social services workforce; for details of the sample see the previous paper by Susan Balloch.

The paper first shows gender differences in the proportion of staff who were senior in each occupational group - social work, domiciliary work and residential work. The proportions of women and men holding qualifications are then compared. The relationship between qualifications and the likelihood of holding a senior post is next examined. Finally, multivariate analysis is used to assess the relative influence of qualifications, gender, age and factors in the work history on the chance of being senior.

Method
Staff were grouped according to their current occupation, whether social work, domiciliary work or residential work, each group including managerial staff. Within each occupational group, the following staff were defined as senior:

Social Work	Senior Social Worker, Area/Team Leader
Domiciliary	Home Care Organiser
Residential	Officers in Charge

In addition, staff working in central/strategic management were defined as senior. The Local Government Management Board codes used to define senior staff are listed in the Appendix. The Appendix also includes tables showing the full information on which the Figures are based.

Results
Figure 1 shows the proportion of staff in senior posts, first for women and men and second for white and black (i.e. not white) staff in each occupational group and among all staff in relation to central management.

Men were more likely to be senior than women in each group and were also more likely to be in central management, the differences being statistically significant (p<.05). White staff were slightly more likely than black to be senior, but here the differences were not great enough to be significant.

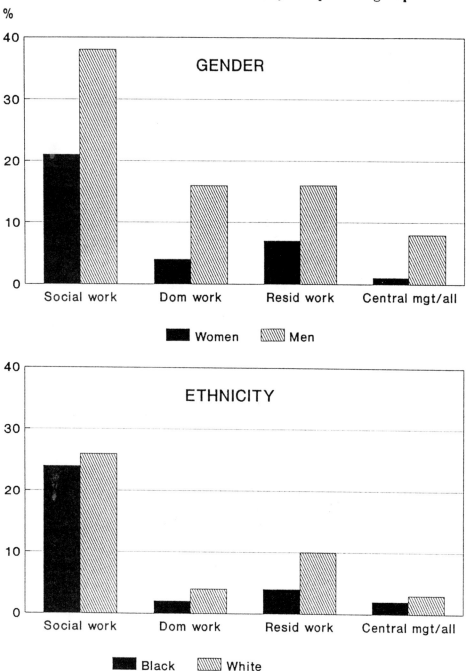

Figure 1
Percentage of staff who were senior, by occupational group

In Figure 2, women and men are compared in terms of whether they held a degree, CQSW (or equivalent) or CSS. Women were much less likely than men to hold a degree, both overall and within each occupational group. Women were also less likely than men to hold a CQSW or CSS, although the gender difference was small among social workers. As shown earlier, very few domiciliary staff held professional qualifications.

Figure 2
Percentage of women and men with qualifications, by occupational group

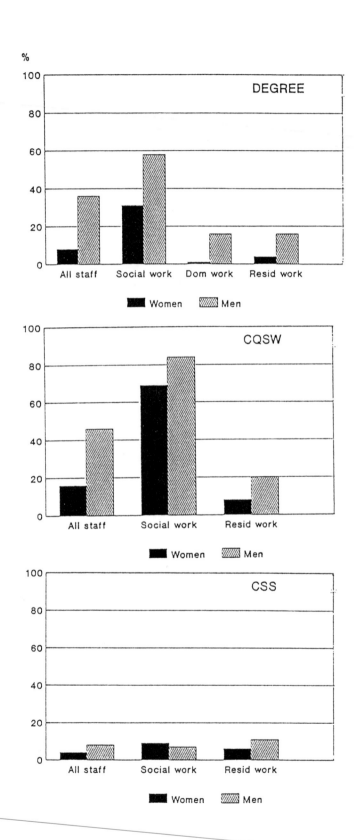

Figure 3
Percentage of staff who were senior, by qualifications

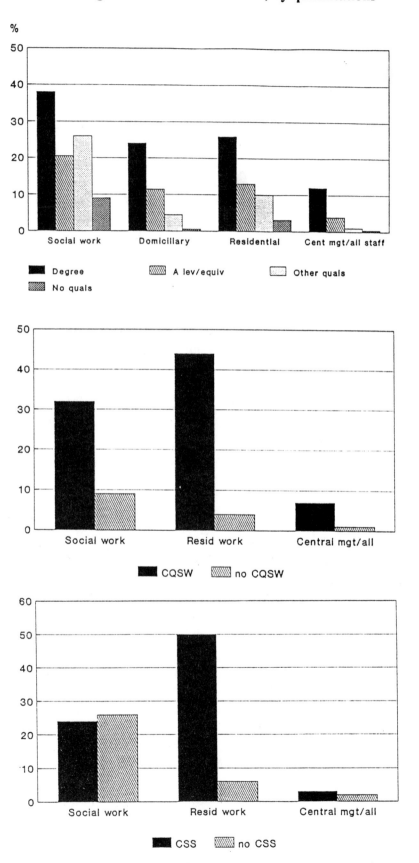

As would be expected, seniority was closely related to qualifications held. Figure 3 shows the percentage of staff who were senior according to educational and professional qualifications.

Staff whose highest educational qualification was a degree or above were most likely to be senior, within each occupation. Among domiciliary and residential staff, those whose highest qualification was A level or equivalent were more likely to be senior than those with O level, GCSE or other. However, among social workers, having an A level as the highest qualification gave no apparent advantage over staff with O levels and equivalent.

Staff holding a CQSW or equivalent were much more likely to be in a senior post than those without, in social work and residential work as well as in central management. For example, a third of staff in social work who held a CQSW were senior compared with less than ten per cent of staff lacking this qualification. CSS was associated with seniority in residential work but not in social work or in central management.

Although we cannot, with these data, be certain that obtaining qualifications preceded promotion for senior staff, this is nevertheless a reasonable assumption to make. On this assumption, the results confirm the importance of both educational and appropriate professional qualifications to career progress. However, the research suggested that other factors might be equally influential. Multivariate analysis was used to compare the separate effects of a large number of variables (see Appendix for variable list).

Table 1 shows the odds ratios of being in a senior post in the best fitting logit models for each occupational group. Gender did not significantly improve the model (nor age, ethnicity, breaks for family care etc.) once the variables shown were included in the model. Information on the relative importance of variables included in each model is given in the Appendix.

For social work, only educational qualifications and years of full time employment in social care improved the model fit significantly. For example, staff whose highest educational qualification was A level or equivalent had odds of only 0.35 of being senior, compared with odds of 1.00 for staff holding a degree. The effect of employment experience was even greater, as indicated by the improvement in model fit. Staff with 10-14 years full time employment in social care had odds of seniority seven times greater than staff with under five years of such employment.

For domiciliary work, the number of jobs in social services had an additional effect, the odds of seniority increasing steeply with number of jobs.

In residential work, holding a CQSW had an effect independently of educational qualifications, in contrast to social work where CQSW had no separate effect. This suggests that in residential work, unlike social work, educational and professional qualifications can be seen as alternative qualifications. Length of full time employment and holding a CQSW were equally important to seniority, educational level less so.

The model for central management differed little from the model for social work, although in this model educational level was more important than length of full time employment.

Table 1
Odds ratios of being in a senior post for staff in three major occupational groups and for all staff in relation to central management

Variable	Social work	Domiciliary work	Residential work	Central management (all staff)
Years full time in social care				
0-4	1.00	1.00	1.00	1.00
5-9	3.31	16.76**	4.28	1.72
10-14	7.27**	19.92*	3.00	2.84
15-19	8.91**	13.91*	30.13**	6.23*
20 or more	21.51**	+	22.92**	18.73**
Educational level				
Degree or above	1.00	1.00	1.00	1.00
A level/equivalent	0.35*	0.16	0.16	0.36
O level/GCSE/other	0.42	0.01*	0.29	0.10**
None	0.03*	0.00**	0.07*	0.04**
CQSW				
Has CQSW			1.00	
No CQSW			0.12**	
Number of jobs in social services				
1		1.00		
2		72.22*		
3		148.77**		
4 or more		>1000.00**		
Null model G^2:	203.6	132.7	174.1	196.7
df:	179	387	296	882
Change in G^2:	-36.1	-66.2	-111.5	-43.4
Change in df:	-7	-9	-8	-7

Difference from reference category statistically significant: *p .05, **p .01.
+ For domiciliary work, 15 or more years was combined into one category.

Conclusions

There is no evidence of direct discrimination against women or black staff; gender per se had no effect on the chance of holding a senior post, once account has been taken of gender differences in the factors associated with seniority. Gender differences in educational and professional qualifications explain a great deal of women's under representation in senior posts. This is encouraging, since women are likely to match men's qualification levels more closely in future, reducing this source of disadvantage and bringing a more equal representation of women in social services management.

There is cause for concern, however, in that it is the length of *full time* rather than total employment in social care which predicts seniority. This suggests that past employment which was part time is less valued for promotion purposes than past full time employment. Since it is mainly women who have periods of part time employment, this would continue to hinder women's career advancement. Yet the family caring work generally undertaken by women while they are employed part time is likely to improve their understanding of clients and hence would bring valuable experience to their role as practitioners in social care.

Discussion

In the discussion, the proportion of social work staff in the sample employed part time in their current job (16 per cent) and the representativeness of the workforce sample were queried. Comparisons with LGMB data indicate, however, that the sample was not untypical of the English workforce.

A question was raised about the relative importance of employment experience compared with qualifications for promotion in social work. It was suggested that for later cohorts of staff qualifications are more essential for promotion than among earlier cohorts. Jay Ginn said that further research is needed on the age at which staff were promoted, on the timing of promotion in relation to obtaining qualifications and on differences between staff cohorts in the factors influencing promotion.

Appendix

Table A1
Percentage of staff in senior positions in each occupation, by gender and ethnicity

	Social work		Domiciliary work		Residential work		Central management (as % of all staff)	
	%	wn	%	wn	%	wn	%	wn
All	25	*180*	4	*388*	9	*301*	2	*891*
Women	21	*134*	4	*375*	7	*251*	1	*772*
Men	38	*45*	16	*14*	16	*50*	8	*119*
Black	24	*34*	2	*37*	4	*64*	2	*138*
White	26	*145*	4	*351*	10	*236*	3	*753*

Table A2
Percentage of staff with qualifications, by gender

Qualifi-cation	All staff		Social work		Domiciliary		Residential	
	women	men	women	men	women	men	women	men
Degree/above	8	36	31	58	1	16	4	16
A level/equiva-lent	10	21	31	23	5	33	7	16
O level/other	34	28	28	13	34	33	40	45
None	47	15	10	7	19	60	50	23
CQSW	16	46	69	84			8	20
CSS	4	8	9	7			6	11
wn	*772*	*119*	*134*	*45*	*375*	*14*	*251*	*50*

Table A3
Percentage of staff in senior positions in each occupation, by educational and professional qualifications

Qualification	Social work	Domiciliary work	Residential work	Central management (as % of all staff)
All staff	25	4	9	2
Degree or above	38	24	26	12
A level/HNC/HND	21	12	13	4
Other educ. quals.*	26	4	10	1
No educ. quals.	9	1	3	<1
CQSW/equiv.	32		44	7
No CQSW/equiv.	9		4	1
CSS	24		50	3
No CSS	26		6	2
wn	*180*	*389*	*301*	*891*

* GCSE, O level, School Leaving Certificate, City & Guilds, clerical or commercial qualifications.

Occupational coding used

Staff with the following LGMB codes were defined as 'senior':

Social work*:   009 010 019 020 028 034** 036 037
Domiciliary: 050
Residential: 102 107 112 117 122 127 133 139 145
Central staff   001 002 003 004 005 007 008 152***

Eleven staff with these codes were reclassified as senior domiciliary staff.
**Classified as senior only if team leader, manager, assistant team manager or senior social worker.*
***Classified as senior only if had a high level of responsibility.*

Variables entered in logit models

AGE5	age (5-year age groups)
AGESC1	age entered social care (5-year age groups)
AGESSD1	age entered social services (5-year age groups)
CQSW	whether had CQSW or equivalent
CSS	whether had CSS
EDLEV	highest educational qualification (not CQSW/CSS)
HOURS	whether employed full time (30+ hours)
TOTSC	years employed in social care (5-year groups)
TOTSCF	full time years employed (5-year groups)
TOTSCP	part time years employed (5-year groups)
SINCESC	years since first social care job (5-year groups)
TOTLASS	years employed in social services (5-year groups)
LASSJOBS	number of jobs in social services (1,2,3,4,5+)
SCJOBS	number of jobs in social care (1,2,3,4,5+)
CBREAK	whether career break taken (maternity leave/family care)
TOTHOME	years of career break (5-year groups)
GENDER	male or female
ETHNIC	black or white

Relative importance of variables in improving model fit (Table 1)

	Gsq	Sig
Social work model		
Years full time in social care	-21.0	.0003
Educational level	-14.1	.0028
Domiciliary work model		
Number of jobs	-31.8	.0000
Educational level	-20.5	.0001
Years full time in social care	-14.0	.0029
Residential work model		
Years full time in social care	-22.7	.0001
CQSW	-14.4	.0001
Educational level	-9.8	.0204
Central management model		
Educational level	-24.7	.0000
Years full time in social care	-18.7	.0009

Workshop 1: Social work education in Europe

Karen Lyons
Principal Lecturer in Social Work, University of East London

Karen Lyons described first some of the variations in social work education and training patterns within the European Union (EU). She then considered the influence of the EU's ERASMUS initiative, which aimed to promote student and staff mobility between European countries, and presented some initial findings from a current EU-funded evaluation of ERASMUS activities.

Variations in social work education in Europe
Structural aspects
Location. Karen Lyons noted that while in the United Kingdom it is taken for granted that social work education takes place in higher education and mainly in the university sector, there is considerable variation in the rest of Europe. In Greece, for example, such education takes place in technical education institutions, and in Sweden traditionally in separate colleges. Where the education takes place has implications for professional identity.

Duration and level. The United Kingdom's two year qualifying training is the shortest. Most other European countries have three year courses, or sometimes four or five years to degree level. In most cases social work training is at undergraduate level. However, Switzerland (a non-EU member but involved in some ERASMUS programmes) has a two year non-graduate diploma and Denmark also has a two or three year qualifying programme. These differences can affect eligibility for certain posts, for example in teaching, or for senior posts in management. There are also implications for professional identity and status, and the development of knowledge and research.

Student characteristics
As in the United Kingdom, social work students across Europe are predominately female and middle class. However, Karen Lyons drew attention to the difference in age of students between the United Kingdom and most other European countries. Denmark and Switzerland recruit older, mature, possibly experienced people, as does the United Kingdom. Elsewhere, the majority of students entering social work education are school leavers between 18 and the early 20s, and suitability for social work is not necessarily assessed as part of selection for courses.

National funding systems and lack of access to grants mean that people from ethnic minority groups are often excluded from social work education. However, in France young unemployed people from ethnic minorities are being trained in youth and community work, and in Sweden and Switzerland asylum seekers have gained places in higher education including social work education.

Epistemological traditions

The construction of courses is affected by different traditions, which can be roughly divided into medical and educational models. The medical model is characterised by a pathologising and problem-centred approach; in the educational model there is greater emphasis on psychology, and on working alongside groups and individuals. There is a large overlap, however, and in Germany, for example, the two strands ('soziale arbeit' and 'sozial pädagoge') are being brought together. Some countries emphasise structural and sociological explanations more than others.

Social work education is affected by different political histories, and how the links between family, the State and professions are viewed. Karen Lyons noted that in the United Kingdom there is much emphasis on anti-discriminatory practice, while elsewhere in Europe the emphasis tends to be more on human rights issues and working with refugees. Attitudes towards sexuality differ: in Denmark, for example, sexuality is seen as a personal issue and not one for professional debate. In the case of disability, too, there are varied traditions - apparent in social work education - of segregation versus integration and paternalism versus user involvement. United Kingdom social work education's commitment to anti-discriminatory practice is invariably a source of debate in ERASMUS networks. Such commitment can be seen as something peculiar to the United Kingdom, or as something from which other European countries can learn.

Practice

Karen Lyons said that there is more emphasis on practice here than in other countries. Although other countries have practice components, these are often well below 50 per cent of the programme content. In Belgium, for example, five year degree courses include two placements of three months each. Also, outside the United Kingdom course requirements tend to be set by the relevant ministry, without formal input from a regulatory body such as we have with CCETSW.

The ERASMUS Programme and United Kingdom evaluation

ERASMUS was introduced in 1987 and will end in 1997. In addition to promoting student and staff mobility between European countries it was also intended to promote harmonisation of the higher education experience of different countries. There is little evidence that this has happened, although there are moves towards identifying commonalities. While the impact of ERASMUS is now being evaluated in the field of social professions, there have been many previous evaluations in other subject areas, and in any case it has already been decided that the programme will be replaced by SOCRATES.

In the United Kingdom an estimated 20 per cent of social work courses have ERASMUS connections, as do one third of Youth and Community courses. Some connections go back to the 1980s but most have developed during the 1990s. British schools of social work tend to be joiners rather than initiators: British schools are in demand not least because foreign students want to improve their English. On the British side, lack of a second European language and the maturity and financial circumstances of British students mean they are less likely to be able to go on placement abroad. Thus, there are some problems in achieving reciprocity. However,

28

inability to speak other languages was not as great a constraint for our students as might be expected, as the common language was so often English and ways around language problems could usually be found. Our two-year courses provide an additional constraint, as ERASMUS rules are that a student cannot go on placement in another country during their first year and students are often reluctant to do so in their final year because of concern about relevance in the job market on return. Yet another constraint is lack of comparable term or semester times, leading to logistical problems.

There have been two examples of joint development within ERASMUS networks leading to nationally recognised awards. The University of Portsmouth and the Skovtofte Socialpaedagogiske Seminarium in Copenhagen have a well-established post-qualifying BA (Hons.) course in European Social Work; and an MA programme in European Social Studies delivered (in English) in Maastricht since 1994 is validated by the University of North London.

Staff mobility has not been very great under ERASMUS. Relatively few people teach for a term at an institution elsewhere in Europe, but they do contribute to joint curriculum development planning. In addition, ERASMUS has provided the opportunity for staff and students to participate in intensive seminars. These take place over a ten-day period with about three institutions and discuss a theme of common concern. For example, a recent one in our network with Italy, Germany and Switzerland discussed working with refugees.

Respondents to a questionnaire about ERASMUS involvement identified the following benefits to United Kingdom social work education:

- broadening of perspectives through placements abroad or participation in the intensive seminars, and through contact with students on placement from elsewhere in Europe
- development of new units with European dimensions, and use of examples from Europe in teaching.

Additionally, in a difficult period for all staff in higher education in the United Kingdom, ERASMUS contacts have provided a new and morale-boosting stimulus.

Karen Lyons said that the aim of SOCRATES, set to replace ERASMUS in 1997, is to widen the European influence on students and courses. There is to be less emphasis on subject-based networks. However, some lessons from ERASMUS do not appear to have been learned - for example the value of intensive seminars. There are real concerns as to how the new programme will work and be funded, and whether it will be possible to maintain the networks which have been established.

Conclusion

British social work education could be viewed as out of step with the rest of Europe in a variety of ways - but not all of these are negative. We have a variety of academic levels, which may be confusing but which does allow a range of opportunities for entering social work and for research. However, some other countries have higher expectations of support and status for those who have completed social work courses; and they do not labour under the sense of public criticism that British social work does, nor are they subject to the same extent to the triple constraints of current Government policies on Europe, on higher education and on welfare services.

Discussion

In the discussion, concerns were expressed about the United Kingdom's narrow and skills-oriented qualification. This was an issue in itself, but also in considering contacts with other European countries. There needed to be more flexibility in accepting qualifications gained elsewhere. At present, for example, a Belgian worker with a social pedagogy qualification (gained over five years) and residential care experience here could not get a fieldwork post in London without taking further courses.

Karen Lyons' point about United Kingdom emphasis on anti-discriminatory work aroused considerable interest. One participant suggested that elsewhere in Europe there was intercultural learning without the underpinning we have; Karen Lyons agreed that there is not the same emphasis on structural theories and issues of power. This led to discussion of the teaching of values in academic courses, and how particular values could be promoted without being (or being seen as) doctrinaire.

References

Barr, H. (1990) *In Europe: 1. Social Work Education and 1992*, CCETSW, London.

Bradley, G. and Harris, R. (1993) 'Social work in Europe: an ERASMUS initiative', *Social Work Education* 12,3: 51-6.

Cannan, C., Berry, L. and Lyons, K. (1992) *Social Work and Europe*, Macmillan, Basingstoke.

Cornwell, N. (1994) 'Social work education and practice sans frontieres', *Issues in Social Work Education* 14,1: 39-52.

Davies Jones, H. (1994) *Social Workers or Social Educators: The international context for developing social care*, International Centre Paper 2, National Institute for Social Work, London.

Davis, A. (1995) 'British social work education and Europe: views from an ERASMUS network', *Social Work in Europe* 2,1: 50-5.

Lorenz, W. (1994) *Social Work in a Changing Europe*, Routledge, London.

Rowlings, C. (1991) 'More than of academic interest: taking a European perspective on social work education', *Issues in Social Work Education* 11,1: 62-68.

Workshop 2: Undertaking a training needs analysis within a social care organisation

Jan Horwath
Lecturer, Department of Sociological Studies, University of Sheffield

What is a training need?

A training need can be defined as the gap in knowledge, skills and attitudes of staff that prevents them effectively meeting organisational objectives. This is a very loose definition and it is not clear who should be defining the need. It may be more constructive to break down the perception of needs into organisational needs, occupational needs and individual needs.

Organisational training needs. An organisational training need exists when there are faults in the system which can be addressed by training; when restructuring or other change is envisaged and staff will need training to prepare for new roles and responsibilities; and when training can removes blocks to the achievement of more desirable objectives (such as a preventative approach to practice).

Occupational training needs. These needs arise because all jobs involve an understanding of the task; acquisition of the knowledge, values and skills to undertake the task; an opportunity to develop these to a proficient level; and an ability to apply them in a more general or specialist way.

Individual training needs. Individuals within an organisation will identify their own training needs, which are likely to reflect concerns for their personal development or career progression as well as their desire to meet organisational objectives.

Balancing the different needs

One of the tensions within social care organisations is the interface between meeting the developmental needs of the individual and the organisation. In many professions there is an acceptance that professionals must have an ongoing commitment to continuing professional development, and to a large extent this has to be a personal, individual commitment. This culture does not exist in social work. A recent experience of interviewing for a trainer's post illustrates this point. Candidates were asked how they kept up to date with current practice issues. The majority stated they did not have time to read social work books but were dependent on one trade journal that is provided free. As one candidate admitted, 'most of the time I skim it and look at the job adverts'.

The development of National Vocational Qualifications and post-qualifying awards should begin to shift the focus of continuing professional development from something that is done to staff, in terms of being sent on courses, to a more proactive process dependent on individual commitment and responsibility. The focus on preparing a portfolio also encourages candidates to take some responsibility for their own learning and development. In addition, this system provides an opportunity for organisations to ensure that they have an appropriately qualified workforce, and goes some way towards enabling individuals to achieve a qualification in their own right.

When is a need a training need?

Much training is delivered as a reactive response to an incident like a child death. This frequently results from an organisation's wish to be seen to respond quickly: training is one of the most visible ways of achieving this. However, this does not take into account the other factors that influence a situation. One of the most complex tasks for both managers and trainers is distinguishing training needs from other factors that impact on workforce effectiveness. It is very common for training to be seen as the panacea for all ills when what is actually required is organisational change or development. In the case of a child death, for example, there may be poor communication between agencies, lack of adequate resources, non-specific guidelines and procedures. Training may have a part to play, but there are clearly other organisational issues which need to be addressed.

Other factors

When faced with a problem within an organisation, or when it is felt that changes are required, it is important to see training in the context of other factors that influence effectiveness. These include:

- adequate staffing
- resources
- relevant policies and procedures
- support and supervision
- an appropriate working environment
- positive emotional climate
- user involvement.

These all impact on achieving the required standard of practice - see Figure 1. If they are not in place training will not be effective in making the progression from actual standard to the required standard. It is too simplistic to consider training as one part of the bridge, presuming all the others are in place. It may well be that training has a role in identifying what is required and what changes need to be made to build the bridge between actual and desired standards. It is for this reason that training cannot be directed purely at front-line workers.

Whose training needs should be considered?

In a climate of limited budgets it is very easy to focus any analysis of training needs on front-line staff. It is often at this level that issues within an organisation become apparent, for example an elderly person dies in their home and it is discovered that an assessment was undertaken but the social worker felt that no services were needed. The immediate response is that staff need training in risk assessment. Little consideration will be given to possible training needs of managers who supervise the staff, or middle and senior managers who determine the budget allocation.

Figure 1

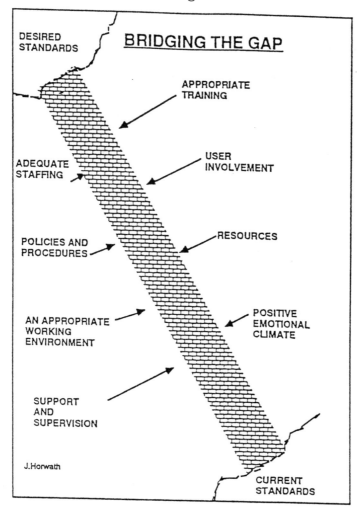

Identifying training needs in the context of change

Trainers, managers and front-line staff need to accept that they are now operating in a climate of continual change. Any change that takes place within an organisation will inevitably raise practice and policy issues that can be addressed by training. Staff at all levels need opportunities to develop their knowledge, values and skills in terms of the tasks they undertake. This is crucial in the promotion and development of good practice.

Senior managers. Training needs analysis must start with senior managers (and, where appropriate, elected members). Managers have a responsibility to ensure a clear understanding throughout the organisation of corporate and departmental objectives, expected service standards, levels of delegated authority, individual tasks and expectations of performance. The following will therefore need to be considered in a training needs analysis of any topic area:

- knowledge of legislation, research and current developments
- relevance of present agency policies, standards and procedures
- the impact on resources and allocation of resources
- the implications of any changes in terms of staff development, supervision and support.

Middle and first-line managers. In the case of these managers, the following will have to be considered in training needs analysis for a topic area:

- knowledge of legislation, research and current practice developments
- knowledge of any new or changed guidelines and procedures
- ability to manage staff and resources within the topic area
- ability to supervise and promote the development of staff in the topic area.

Front-line staff. Training needs analysis for front-line staff will need to consider:

- knowledge of legislation, research and current practice as these impact on their role
- understanding of new or changed guidelines and procedures, and their roles and responsibilities within this context
- understanding of practice implications and their knowledge, skills and values within this context
- ability to work in partnership with service users in light of the service developments.

Techniques to use in identifying agency training needs

Feedback from training courses. At the end of training courses, participants are regularly asked to complete 'happy sheets' designed to enable trainers to evaluate the effectiveness of the training. A section of the form can be devoted to establishing participants' views on their future training needs.

Questionnaires. These can be distributed to staff at various levels within the organisation to establish their views of the training needs of the organisation.

Roxby's planning model for group development. A number of small groups can be set up and individuals asked to 'quick think' what they feel are the agency's training needs. These ideas can then be collated and priority given to those that are mentioned most frequently.

Critical incident analysis. A group of staff can be asked to consider a situation when the workforce did not function well as a result of lack of knowledge and skills. The group then analyses what went wrong and tries to identify the lack of knowledge and skills that led to the incident.

Interviews. The trainer can meet with key personnel at various levels within the organisation to identify what they feel are the training needs for all the different staff groups. This is a very effective way of getting different perspectives on the knowledge, values and skills required by different staff groups, but it can be time-consuming.

Workplace demands. This occurs when staff identify a need and are proactive in bringing it to the trainer's attention.

Development groups. The 'connectedness' of each tier in the organisation can be reinforced by arranging for a development group consisting of staff at all levels to meet, develop and evaluate the training and development strategy. For example, in Nottinghamshire the Area Child Protection Committee wanted to develop a training strategy for post-registration working. A group was set up of personnel from a variety of disciplines and at different levels within their organisations. The group was able to identify the issues that those working in this area encountered. The roles of front-line practitioners and of managers were explored from different perspectives and a training strategy developed that recognised the relationships among all those involved in child protection, at the front line and within the management structure. As managers were present from different tiers within the organisations they were able to convince their colleagues of the relevance of the ensuing training.

Techniques to use in identifying individual training needs

Job description and specification. One method of identifying need is to consider what is required of individuals and how they and/or their manager rate their ability to undertake the job. This process can identify training needs at a variety of levels, from basic acquisition to developing specialist skills.

Staff appraisal. This is a system for monitoring the development of staff members by assessing what they have achieved and identifying areas for further development in terms of agency, job and individual needs. It is usually undertaken by a superior, frequently the individual's manager.

Supervision. Part of the supervisor's role is to take responsibility for the supervisee's development. Supervisors should be continually identifying training needs and prioritising these with their staff.

Personal profiling. This involves on-going monitoring of an individual's development, taking into account their job, their own developmental needs and their career ambitions. It is a tool for considering the needs of the individual as a whole, and provides a framework for taking a strategic approach incorporating training, supervision and work experience. In Sheffield Family and Community Services this system has been operating for some time. Every member of staff has a profile, from the Director to front-line staff. The profile acts as a tool for monitoring an individual's learning needs, identifying appropriate methods of meeting these needs, considering ways of facilitating the learning into practice and evaluating effectiveness through supervision. As the profile is a document for staff members throughout their time in the Department, if someone changes job their learning needs can be reassessed on the basis of their prior learning. As the profile is regularly revisited and updated during supervision it reinforces a commitment to an ongoing process of staff development. It has the additional benefit of enabling all those involved in the organisation to take a systematic approach towards learning and development, and emphasises the connection between tiers in the organisation, reminding both the individual and the manager of their roles and responsibility towards staff development.

Prioritising training needs

Any training needs analysis will highlight a whole range of different training needs within an organisation. It is very unlikely that they can all be met. Consequently, they will have to be prioritised. This should be done in conjunction with senior managers, thereby ensuring that they take some ownership of the ensuing training strategy. The needs can be broken down into *essential, highly desirable* and *desirable*. Once agreement has been reached about the level to which training can be developed then it is helpful for the trainer and managers to agree a service level agreement which makes explicit their commitment to seeing the training strategy through and reinforces their ownership of the training.

Issues

The position of the trainer and the training department. The approach described above is in many ways an ideal model. It assumes that the trainer and the training section hold positions within the organisation that enable them to liaise with senior managers and undertake this systematic approach. However, many trainers are not in this position. Where they are marginalised, they may provide training that is based on assessing the needs of their 'allies', or training that is based on their own perceptions of what is required by the organisation. At the other extreme are trainers who have little control or power and are expected to provide training based on the requests of managers. In these cases trainers are in no position to undertake a training needs analysis that will bring about effective change.

User involvement. A systematic approach towards training and development must consider the perspectives of service users. I am currently involved in the development of a child care training strategy which, as part of the training needs analysis, asked service users what they expected from social services staff. Those consulted were adults and young people who had been involved in the care system and experienced child protection investigations. There were some very positive benefits, ensuring that the training programmes reflected a user perspective. Indeed, some of the service users have been trained as trainers and are now involved in delivering the training.

The feedback from participants is that this method of training, needs analysis and course delivery raises their awareness of the user perspective and the importance, tensions and issues of working in partnership with children and their families.

Motivation of staff. It is all too easy, when considering training needs analysis, to presume that staff are ready to discuss their training needs. Traditions develop within organisations that can result in some middle and senior managers feeling unable to admit to a need for training since this may be seen as a weakness. There is often an unspoken assumption that once an individual has moved from a practitioner role to a managerial role they do not require training other than management development. It is consequently important when considering training needs to consider how different staff groups within the organisation may perceive training, and address their concerns accordingly.

Staff such as home care workers are not easily available to discuss their training needs; and their supervisors - because of the number they manage - may not be able to identify needs using the methods outlined above. In addition, many of these staff may be afraid to admit to training needs as training is perceived as intimidating and formal, and conjures up images of back-to-school for talk and chalk.

This was very clearly put on an evaluation form by a domestic worker in a young children's centre who had completed a course on child protection:

I was so scared about coming on this course I had sleepless nights. I was scared I would be put on the spot and made to look a fool. I cannot read and write very well and was frightened everyone would know. This course has made me see training very differently. I can't wait for another course.

Discussion

Participants raised some continuing concerns. These included, for example, how senior managers and councillors could be encouraged to accept training (suggestion: call it a seminar and get in a big name) and how staff could be encouraged to keep up to date with current research (suggestion: get on free mailing list for Joseph Rowntree Foundation *Findings* series). Many of the concerns expressed, however, were about the implications of current circumstances for trainers and the training role. Among these were:

- the pressures to focus on 'measurable outcomes'
- the necessity of involving service users in evaluation, but the likelihood of negative responses in light of service cutbacks
- the danger that training needs analysis will be seen as tokenism when resources are being reduced
- the additional issues arising in planning training for particular units which will be in competition with voluntary or private sector agencies
- how managers can be enabled to become staff developers when they feel 'under siege'
- the possible need to defuse stress among some workers caused by competence-based approaches
- the difficulty of doing useful work when staff development units are in a state of flux, or under threat of being contracted out.

There was considerable interest in the Sheffield profiling system outlined by Jan Horwath. She reported that the system had not yet been implemented in the home care service. In other parts of the Department she thought that there probably was actual use of the profiles in about 60 per cent of cases.

Workshop 3: Evaluating professional nursing training for the impact on practice

Sue Davies
Lecturer (Health Services Research), Department of Sociological Studies,
University of Sheffield

This paper explores some of the methodological issues associated with attempts to evaluate the effects on nursing practice of continuing professional education. The paper draws on the experiences of a research team at the University of Sheffield who are currently engaged in a two year project to evaluate pre- and post-registration education for the care of older people. The research is funded by the English National Board for Nursing, Midwifery and Health Visiting (ENB) and the project team is multidisciplinary. The diversity of the team, both in terms of practice discipline and methodological orientation, has had an important influence on the choice of research design.

The project aims to determine the extent to which educational programmes in nursing prepare practitioners to promote autonomy and independence for older people in their care and includes three separate but overlapping phases.

Phase One is a national survey of centres providing pre- and post-registration education to identify aspects of educational programmes which relate to the promotion of autonomy and independence for older people. Data collection has involved content analysis of a sample of curriculum documents for a range of educational programmes and a detailed questionnaire completed by course leaders describing how the curriculum is operationalised.

Phase Two is a national survey of nursing homes in three regions (n = 1000). A self-completion questionnaire was sent to each nurse manager asking for detailed information on the grade and qualifications of nursing staff within each home and inviting the senior nurse to complete a scale devised to measure resident autonomy within continuing care settings. Our intention was to identify any association between the educational preparation of nursing staff and a measure of resident autonomy and independence.

Phase Three was planned as a randomised controlled trial to evaluate a short course in the Nursing Care of Elderly People (ENB course 941). We intended to complement data from this with semi-structured interviews with course members, their managers and the course teacher.

Challenges
Whereas phases one and two have proceeded relatively smoothly, phase three has encountered a number of methodological challenges which have ultimately caused the research team to abandon the attempt to set up a randomised controlled trial and switch to a quasi-experimental approach. The decision to attempt a randomised

controlled trial was influenced by the need to demonstrate outcomes in relation to the quality of care provided to older people (as specified by the ENB). Furthermore, within the context of evidence based purchasing, many managers are seeking demonstrable outcomes for their investment in continuing professional education. However, the literature suggests a general absence of research based evidence to demonstrate a change in clinical practice following completion of a course. With a few exceptions, much of the research evaluating nurse education has focused upon the subjective perceptions of course members. The plan to conduct a randomised controlled trial was an attempt to move knowledge forward in this field and see if it was possible to identify a causal link between education and a change in practice.

The trial was designed to test the following research hypothesis:

> Nurses who have completed ENB course 941 are more likely to promote autonomy and independence in their practice with older people than nurses who have not undertaken the programme.

In order to test this hypothesis, we needed to identify two groups of nurses: the experimental group who would undertake the programme and a control group who would also undertake course 941 but outside the timeframe of the study. The knowledge, attitudes and practice of both groups would then be measured before the introduction of the independent variable to the experimental group and again after the experimental group had completed the course. Instrumentation included a self-completion questionnaire which we proposed to administer to both groups before and after the programme. We also planned to observe a sub-sample of both groups in practice, again before and after the 941 programme using a structured rating scale. The challenges in setting up the trial included:

- randomisation of potential course members to the control and experimental groups
- manipulation of a standard intervention
- measurement of dependent variables.

Randomisation to the control and experimental groups
In order to explore the feasibility of the trial, 47 nurse managers who had previously nominated nurses to attend course 941 were identified via course leaders and all were interviewed by telephone. The purpose of the study was explained in detail and managers were asked to consider whether they could identify all of the nurses whom they planned to nominate to course 941 during the coming year. They were also asked to consider whether they would allow the research team to allocate randomly from this list either to the next 941 programme or to the one following. The majority of managers were very interested in the study and agreed, in principle, to the idea of random allocation. However, the feasibility of this approach was affected by a number of factors:

- changes in the system of contracting resulting from Working Paper 10 reducing the number of nominations to the programme
- managers' perceptions of the effect which the trial would have on service provision if two nurses from the same practice area were allocated to the same programme
- lack of a standard process for nominating nurses to undertake programmes

- nominees' reluctance to agree to random allocation.

More general problems included difficulties in determining when individual programmes would start and end. Many programmes were in the process of being modularised with the result that the programme completion date fell outside the time frame of the study. This reduced the pool of potential recruits.

Lack of a standard intervention

Classical experimental design depends upon the manipulation of the independent variable (in this case course 941) according to a standard protocol. It is important that all subjects allocated to the experimental group receive the same intervention delivered in a similar way. We had assumed that each 941 programme would be fairly similar to other 941 programmes and had not anticipated the variation in course length, style and content that we discovered when we looked at the programmes in more detail.

Measurement of dependent variables

In common with so many of the concepts which are central to nursing practice, autonomy and independence are abstract ideas which almost defy definition. However, it was essential for us to operationalise these terms in a way that would make them observable and measurable within the context of the randomised controlled trial. At an early stage we decided that it would not be possible to measure autonomy and independence from the patient's perspective and that we would have to focus upon the nurse's practice as the outcome measure. In searching for relevant indicators of a change in nursing practice, we tried to focus upon aspects of care-giving which empirical evidence suggests are important to older people themselves.

Following an extensive review of the literature we decided that in both the development of the observation schedule and the self-completion questionnaire we would focus on the extent to which the nurse:

- offered the patient choice in relation to day to day activities
- provided information or explanation about care
- attempted to elicit feedback from the patient in relation to actions taken or care given
- attempted to protect and respect the patient's privacy
- encouraged participation in care planning
- took action to promote patient safety
- took action to encourage independence in the activities of daily living.

We also looked for evidence of reciprocity within the nurse-patient relationship, such as giving personal information and appropriate use of humour.

Both the research instruments have had to be developed from scratch and the timescale of the project has allowed only limited tests of reliability and validity. We have therefore felt it necessary to maintain detailed fieldnotes during each period of observation to support the ratings for each event. However, in reviewing these fieldnotes we have begun to feel that they provide vital information for interpreting the phenomena we are studying. It may be that this reflects the stage of development of the research instruments and the need for further development and pilot work before the tool can be used to 'measure' aspects of nursing practice. An alternative explanation is that the interactions and events which we are observing are so complex that we will never be able to reduce them meaningfully to points on a rating scale.

Conclusion

Our experience suggests that the current organisation and structure of continuing professional education in nursing poses a number of barriers to the successful conduct of a randomised controlled trial. Furthermore, the appropriateness of this to evaluate education for health and social care practice is questionable. Many of the interventions which education for such practice aims to promote, for example interventions to enable self-determination among older people - the focus of the study outlined here - take place within a complex framework of social interaction. In such a context and in the absence of additional sources of information, the randomised controlled trial may prove too reductionist an approach for a true evaluation to emerge. As social researchers, we may have to resist pressure to perceive the randomised controlled trial as the gold standard against which all attempts at evaluation will be judged.

Discussion

Participants were particularly interested in the methodological issues raised by Sue Davies' presentation. Discussion concerned the general problems of trying to apply randomised controlled trials to non-medical questions, and the specific challenges in this research of defining autonomy and/or independence and then finding appropriate measures or indicators - especially when frail older people in residential settings were involved.

Workshop 4: Management training: the role of open learning

Giles Darvill
Consultant, National Institute for Social Work

Giles Darvill presented findings from his evaluation of a new two-year management training programme for health and social services managers, where local courses use open learning materials specially developed by the Open University.

He noted that until recently management education in the social services had been based on general management. It had been delivered to the workbase by universities and other external agencies, taught directly or through distance learning, and assessed academically. There had been poor links with the workbase for help with learning 'inputs' and for developing outcomes.

He noted that there were now more courses geared specifically to social services management. One in particular, Health and Social Services Management (HSSM), is for joint training for middle managers. It is delivered on agency site or externally, by a university or in-house team or a mix of these. It is based on open learning materials and can be assessed academically and/or in terms of competences. The links with the workbase can be much better than in other more traditional courses, but there are still some problems.

His evaluation has been looking at input components and workbase outcomes, rather than the learning experience as such. The evaluation relates to three courses: two of these are in locality A and one in locality B. In locality A, one course is an HSSM course with ten candidates; the other is a parallel course for seven first-line managers. In both cases most students are health services managers. In locality B the HSSM course has eight managers each from health and social services. In both areas the course is presented on site by in-house teams.

The evaluation methodology used has been interactive and developmental. It has included interviews, attendance at meetings, meetings with service users and use of questionnaires. Giles Darvill has informally interviewed tutors and participants; attended course meetings; and administered questionnaires to candidates. In locality A he has also had meetings with service users, and in locality B attended planning and management review meetings.

Inputs and course processes
The main course inputs have been studying open learning materials with associated workshops, 'action learning' discussions, one-to-one sessions with National Vocational Qualification (NVQ) assessors and mentors, and (locality A only) help from a service users' panel.

There has been general satisfaction with the course inputs, but there has been serious competition for time, with learning sets taking over in locality A and having to be suppressed. Materials and their concepts and theories have not been greatly used. One of the locality A courses made more effective use of the users' panel than the other one did. The highest value was given to one-to-one help, especially from NVQ advisers and assessors. In general, NVQ is valued, although there have been some grumbles about NVQ 'fussiness'.

Looking at middle managers, and referring to course components:

- A wide range of components scored highly and there were few low scoring components.
- Interpersonal components were valued above materials.
- No weak area of course content was identified when evaluated for usefulness against a range of key management tasks (such as planning, personnel work). For each task area, the course was a lot of use or some use to the majority.

Almost everyone found the course of considerable help in a small number of main tasks, rather than there being clusters of managers receiving a lot of help with a lot of tasks and others no help at all. There is some evidence that women used the course more fully than men did; and although there was variable success with NVQs there was some evidence that women did better than men.

Candidates were asked to rank seven different types of help they received in achieving two key result areas (low=1, high = 6). The table below shows average ratings for middle managers and for first-line managers:

	middle managers (n=10)	first-line managers (n=7)
the management course	3.45	3.30
other training received at any time	3.45	3.35
help from managers at own level	3.45	2.90
help from more senior managers	3.25	3.80
help from subordinate managers and their staff	3.25	3.50
agency guidelines, procedures, etc.	3.20	2.90
additional resources	2.95	2.60

Workbase outcomes

Workbase inputs especially from senior managers and previous training score as highly as this sophisticated course, and this is especially the case for first-line managers. Middle managers seem to need the distance from the workbase more for their immediate learning, but making the links back remains problematic.

The major issue appears to be the poor links between personal development and strategic organisational development. Giles Darvill suggested that this was particularly disappointing because NVQ standards are made for organisational development as well as personal development.

He noted that agencies are beginning to respond to HSSM courses on a 'middle-out' basis. Groups of middle managers find themselves in the same forums and their joint learning can then begin to make a collective impact on the agency. Thus far this development has been internal to social services or to health, not joint.

Senior managers and other middle managers pick up the learning more organically, for example from acting as assessors or mentors. Transfer of learning is, however, more obvious from the middle to below: candidates use aspects of HSSM to develop their teams.

The attempt to involve service users in locality A was an excellent one, and many lessons were learned and applied. Overall, however, the service users themselves felt let down.

Reflections and lessons
Course tutors have had a challenging time. They have had continuously to reframe their concept of a workbased open learning course, working to get a better balance between action learning and materials about concepts and theories, and trying to make NVQ processes helpful and not an obstacle. Timing has been found to be important, and also how portfolio-building is approached.

Ideally, there need to be better links from the outset between the workbase and the learning programme. More attention needs to be paid to how learning can spread across the organisation smoothly and effectively, including for example programmes and workshops which will help to draw on and disseminate the intended and actual learning of managers attending courses. Service users, like candidates, need to be associated more with the development of an agency's overall strategy as a frame for the course.

In-house sited and delivered programmes so far seem best, from the experience of localities A and B. Universities are, however, learning to deliver in-house so maybe the best of both worlds is available, especially if materials can be made more useful for workbased development.

Giles Darvill pointed to the use of joint accreditation: the same material was being assessed for NVQ, academic, professional social work and professional management qualifications. Were there lessons here for the future of the DipSW and NVQ level 4 in social care? What about in-house assessment?

Discussion
Participants raised questions about recruitment to courses from both health and social services. One local authority was said to have had great difficulty in establishing joint arrangements. Giles Darvill agreed that there were many constraints. Good relationships were required before such recruitment would work, and sometimes it took two or three years to get results. One of the participants described a joint health/social services course some years ago which was to consider new ways of

delivering services to people with learning difficulties. When it came to putting a concrete project into effect, senior management support from both sides was required - but lacking.

It was generally accepted that people do like working together, and appreciate the opportunity to talk and share common problems. However, courses need to go beyond this, with theory brought into the discussion of everyday problems, with course materials and course leaders making the links between theory and practice quite explicit. The skills of the person running the course were seen as crucial.

Participants asked how self-contained course material needed to be, how flexible, and how easily brought up to date. Some concern was expressed about NVQ levels. Where level 4 material was used it was found to be insufficiently challenging, and even level 5 was rather basic. One participant wondered how crucial the particular material used was to outcomes: is it the process that matters most? Giles Darvill said that there were examples of courses without materials but such courses probably experienced more drop-out.

Workshop 5: The future of the Diploma in Social Work

Mick Farrant
Acting Assistant Director (Education and Training), Central Council for
Education and Training in Social Work

Jenny Weinstein
Project Manager, Central Council for Education and Training in Social Work

In this Workshop, Mick Farrant discussed developments in the Diploma in Social
Work (DipSW) and issues arising from current arrangements and from changes in the
wider context. Jenny Weinstein then outlined the aims and outcomes of the Review of
the DipSW, and proposed developments.

Mick Farrant said that the acid tests for the future of the DipSW were whether it was a
qualification desired by employers and by students, and whether it was a programme
which universities and employers found attractive to provide.

There was evidence that it was a qualification desired by employers. For the last three
years over 90 per cent of people gaining a DipSW/ CQSW/CSS obtained a job in
social services within six months of completion; this was in marked contrast to, for
example, teachers. Private social care agencies such as Reed, mainly in London,
employ over 1400 'temporary' qualified social workers, many of whom have
qualifications gained outside the United Kingdom. Predictions that S/NVQs would
replace the DipSW have not so far happened. Indeed, the CCETSW NVQ registrations
for 1994 and 1995 were, at 6,800 and 6,500 respectively, well below expectations.

As far as students were concerned, the ratio of applicants to places has remained at
around three to one. Intakes to DipSW and its predecessor qualifications have varied
between about 4,800 and 5,600 over the last ten years. This contrasts with nurses, for
example, where intakes of 37,000 in 1984 decreased to 17,000 in 1995 and are
expected to decline to 14,000 in 1996.

Since 1986, intakes and awards have been as follows:

year	intake	awards
1986	4827	4169
1987	4945	4166
1988	4910	4279
1989	5042	4354
1990	4818	4333
1991	4968	4415
1992	5607	4453
1993	5502	4224
1994	5169	4707
1995	5067	4659

The above gives a total of 50,855 registrations, an average of 5,086 per year; and 43,759 awards, an average of 4,376 per year.

Supply, demand and problems of the present system
CCETSW has a United Kingdom target of an intake of 5,500 and output of 5,000. However, plan as much as we like, decisions about supply of and demand for qualified social workers are made by a variety of different stakeholders who may have very different agendas, and agendas which are changing rapidly. There is thus no central locus which can control supply and demand. Stakeholders can only play their part and exhort others. To date there is no suggestion that social work should go down the route being followed by nurses.

CCETSW cannot control who is employed as a social worker: there is no qualification requirement, except in Northern Ireland, and throughout the United Kingdom as regards Mental Health Officer/Approved Social Worker.

CCETSW contributes to the funding of training through its contributions to student bursaries, placements and programme management. (For example, it funds about 20 per cent of students on postgraduate DipSW programmes.) This is only a minority of total funding, however, which weakens CCETSW's influence on university and agency decisions about involvement in training. In 1992 CCETSW Council alerted government to the increasing problems of the funding system - problems which are becoming more acute.

Developments since 1986
- In 1995 the number of applicants per place began to decline.
- From a peak in 1992/3 it looks like registrations are beginning to dip.
- Employment-based routes (i.e. secondment) recruited 1,466 in 1986 but were down to 800 by 1994.
- Excluding Probation students, the comparable sources of funding for students in 1986 declined from 52 per cent by employers (48 per cent by grants/bursaries) to 20 per cent by employers (80 per cent grants/bursaries) by 1994.
- An increasing number of DipSW programmes have become either DipHE or undergraduate degrees, attracting mandatory local education authority grants. While to an extent this dealt with problems attached to discretionary grant funding, it has been replaced with another problem: increasing student poverty.
- CCETSW's bursaries have increased from 772 (1986) to 1,171 (1994). However, the available number of bursaries is beginning to decline gradually as costs increase without corresponding increases in CCETSW's budget for these.
- The student wastage rate (i.e. students not completing the course) at the beginning of the period was in the region of seven per cent and by the end of the period estimated at 13 per cent.

The changes in probation training with its removal of 300 places has not yet had drastic effects on the DipSW system. Problems related to provision of placements have not been so severe as to collapse the system. Local government reorganisation has not as yet resulted in damage. However, there are a number of changes in the provision of the training system which are just around the corner which need addressing. Unless this is done, DipSW will be under threat, not because employers do not want qualified social workers but because there are not sufficient numbers of qualified people available. If they are not available, employers will turn elsewhere for qualified staff. This may lead to further decreases in provision and a downward spiral.

Immediate issues

The increasing wastage rate of students. Is this related to the increasing phenomenon of student poverty? Social work students are much older than most students on local education authority grants and thus, with more commitments, will find it increasingly harder to manage.

Secondment by employers. Such secondment has virtually collapsed as employers find it cheaper to recruit qualified social workers who are trained at others' expense. Together with the point above, this is likely to depress student registrations.

Obtaining placements. Placements are becoming more difficult to obtain, even where Department of Health funding is available to statutory agencies.

Funding. This is becoming an increasing issue for all programme providers.

Wider issues

The 'revolution' in vocational training as evidenced by SCOTVEC and NCVQ has been slowly working its way up the system from level 2 to level 4 and beyond. So far as social work training is concerned, the latest manifestation is NCVQ/SCOTVEC approval of level 4 qualifications in Social Care to join those in Criminal Justice and also Special Needs Housing and Community Work. Where does the DipSW fit into this system - if at all? The issue is not about the level 4 qualification being a 'competitor' for the DipSW but rather the lack of resolution of the conflict between *professional, vocational* and *academic* education and training systems. Social work training is a minor player in this area. Indeed, CCETSW has tried to work within all systems but this has not prevented problems.

Changes in funding for higher education, and decisions made by individual universities and agency partners, pose a threat to the DipSW. DipSW programmes are seen as more expensive than other programmes in the 'Professions Allied to Medicine' category. It is thus possible that some institutions will decide to move to these less costly programme/degree options. Indeed, plans for the development of 'social welfare' degrees indicate that this may be about to occur.

Other imminent changes in the higher education funding system include the impact of the Research Assessment Exercise on social work programmes, the review of post-graduate provision and the Dearing Report on the future of funding in higher education.

Review of the DipSW

Jenny Weinstein noted that 'social work', as an activity, has changed radically over the last three decades. Education has traditionally lagged behind practice, but change is now so rapid that we cannot afford to be complacent about this. Since the late 1980s the Government has been challenging the monopoly of the professions and the preparation of professionals in higher education institutions. Recent examples are the withdrawal of Probation from DipSW by the Home Office, and the initiative to train teachers in the classroom. More significantly, the Government's National Standards programme has been extended to higher levels, bringing professional training and qualifications within its remit and within Government targets.

The swing towards employment interests and assessment of competence in the workplace was and is anathema to many professional bodies and academic institutions. Critics question the efficacy of the assessment process, particularly in relation to the acquisition of underpinning knowledge and because of the complexity of most professional activity and the importance of developing critical, analytic and reflective thought.

It is against this backdrop that the Review of the DipSW took place, at very short notice and within a strictly limited timescale. The extension of the remit of industry lead bodies to higher levels led to the employment interests on our own Occupational Standards Council - the Care Sector Consortium (CSC) - threatening to move into the social work arena. The risks were real because of the comparative weakness of social work as a profession: no qualification requirement for appointment as a social worker, no protection of title, not a fully graduate profession, having only a two-year training, and not having a regulatory body.

CCETSW confronted these problems by going into partnership with CSC to review the DipSW. The agreed aims were to develop draft national occupational standards for beginning social workers one year into practice, and to review and revise the statement of requirements (the knowledge, values and skills required for the award of DipSW) based on the draft occupational standards.

CCETSW's aims were to:

- defend the DipSW as *the* professional qualification for a career in social work, firmly rooted in Higher Education but also bridging the professional and vocational frameworks
- secure the DipSW within the progressive continuum of qualification - vocational qualification, post qualifying and advance awards - and particularly to articulate a bridge with the emerging level 4 NVQ qualifications in care
- establish more consistent standards at outcome for the DipSW
- promote more flexible access to the DipSW
- achieve contemporary relevance for the DipSW in the context of changing needs, legislation and service delivery throughout the United Kingdom.

Outcome of the Review
The outcome of the functional analysis process, which sought to include social workers in all parts of the United Kingdom, from all sectors and settings, working with the full range of service users, was that there are *six core functions of social work*. It was decided that a student should be required to show evidence of possessing them all before being awarded the DipSW. The language of functional analysis and vocational qualifications was not used for the DipSW because it was feared that this would be seen as reducing the complexities of social work to a mechanistic list of tick boxes. It

was also considered essential to avoid a detailed desegregation of competences in favour of a holistic assessment which would be more appropriate for the award of a professional qualification.

The DipSW competences contain complex concepts such as rights, risks and change. The core tasks require a reflective analytical approach, incorporating a highly developed level of interpersonal skills, professional judgement and personal and professional values and integrity.

The Review produced a knowledge base related to the core competences and a set of values requirements which underpin the whole social work task. These must be integrated into the core competences and demonstrated throughout the student's practice. A holistic assessment of the student's progress is undertaken at an intermediate stage and at the end of the programme. If at any stage there are serious concerns that the student is not a suitable candidate to undertake the social work role, there must be procedures for terminating their continuation on the programme.

CCETSW continues to argue for a three-year training leading to a fully graduate profession, compatibility with elsewhere in Europe and a better trained workforce. However, in light of Government opposition to this, post-qualifying education and training combined with a high standard of induction, support and supervision for newly qualified staff is essential if standards are to be maintained.

Proposed developments
Pathways. Given the restrictions of a two-year programme of study, the debate about whether to provide generic or specialist training has been ongoing for many years. The new DipSW offers a choice for both programmes and students to pursue either general or particular pathways. Guidance for Adult Services/Community Care and for Child Care/Residential Child Care has already been published by CCETSW. Guidance is in preparation for Sensual Impairment and there are plans for guidance on a Criminal Justice pathway.

Interprofessional education. Joint or shared learning with other professions is being developed. A programme in the Midlands is offering a pathway on visual impairment; those who follow this will gain both a DipSW and a Rehabilitation Officer qualification. A programme in the North is exploring the potential for a Mental Health pathway which will be shared with registered nurses specialising in mental illness. Shared modules for occupational therapists and social workers are also being explored.

Links with level 4 S/NVQ. Pathways also offer a way of developing bridges between the vocational and the academic frameworks. For example, modules from a particular pathway may provide the underpinning knowledge for a level 4 candidate. Indicative links have already been made in the existing pathways guidance. Alternatively, a holder of a level 4 award may be able to claim credit towards DipSW. CCETSW is undertaking a project with DipSW programme providers and assessment centres to explore these possibilities with a view to issuing further guidance.

Open Learning. The Open University has been funded by the Department of Health to develop an open learning DipSW Programme. They are currently in partnership with the Northern Ireland Eastern Board, Barnardos and Wolverhampton Social Services. In the initial stages they will only take students from the agency partners, who will have to take full responsibility for the practice learning side of the programme. In the future, they hope to take students who are not necessarily working in a partner agency, or in any agency, using innovative approaches to placement provision.

In addition, many mainstream programmes are offering parts of their programme or particular modules using open learning materials. Both the Open University and the Open Learning Foundation have produced helpful publications advising on good practice in using open learning materials.

Assessment of Prior Experience and Learning (AP(E)L). The revised DipSW allows credit to be awarded for any part or, if appropriate, for all the award. There are currently many social care staff with considerable experience and in-service training who want to access DipSW but could not afford a full two-year programme. There are also people from other professions undertaking care management and other social work roles who would value a DipSW but who do not want to repeat learning which they already achieved in their own training. Initial guidance is being issued by CCETSW on good practice in awarding credit to DipSW students for AP(E)L.

Conclusion

Jenny Weinstein concluded by noting that although DipSW is clearly in a much more competitive market than it used to be, it is still recognised as *the* qualification for a career in social work. The Review has brought the requirements up to date, preparing people to work in current social work settings. The flexibility of the revised qualification will undoubtedly make it more attractive to both potential candidates and sponsoring employers. However, we must engage in ongoing critical evaluation of DipSW to ensure its continued relevance to current needs of service users and modes of service delivery.

Conference participants

Shama Ahmed	Central Council for Education and Training in Social Work
Toby Andrew	National Institute for Social Work
Judith Avill	Sheffield Family and Community Services
Susan Balloch	National Institute for Social Work
Margaret Barnes	Sefton Social Services Department
Michael Branicki	Hampshire Social Services Department
Robin Burgess	Hounslow Social Services Department
Lesley Burt	Hampshire Social Services Department
Ruth Chadwick	Department of Health Research and Development Division
Liz Chidgey	Essex Social Services Department
John Clements	Hertfordshire Social Services Department
Jim Connelly	Department of Health Social Services Inspectorate
Phaik Connor	Ealing Social Services Department
Richard Cox	Royal National Institute for the Blind
Andrew Crocker	Devon Social Services Department
David Crosbie	Department of Health Social Services Inspectorate
Giles Darvill	National Institute for Social Work
Barbara Davey	National Institute for Social Work
Anne Davies	Partnerships in Action Ltd.
Carolyn Davies	Department of Health Research and Development Division
Sue Davies	University of Sheffield
Margaret Dempsey	Central Council for Education and Training in Social Work
Steve Dobson	Central Council for Education and Training in Social Work
Geraldine Doherty	Central Council for Education and Training in Social Work
Mick Farrant	Central Council for Education and Training in Social Work
Julie Featherstone	Practice Teacher
Rose Franks	East Sussex Social Services Department
Judith Freedman	Surrey Staff Development
P.Frost	Brighton University
Jay Ginn	National Institute for Social Work
Jenny Gray	Department of Health Social Services Inspectorat
Tony Hall	Central Council for Education and Training in Social Work
Roger Halls	Cambridgeshire Social Services Department
Judy Hamblin	Sheridan Systems Ltd.
Sharon Hamlin	Hillingdon Social Services Department
Phillip Heasman	Christ Church College
Jan Horwath	University of Sheffield
David Jones	Central Council for Education and Training in Social Work
Val Jones	Southampton Institute
Joe Lake	London Borough of Greenwich Training
Karen Lyons	University of East London

Peter Marsh   University of Sheffield
Anita Marsland   Wigan Social Services Department
Claire Maxwell   Northumberland Social Services Department
Kate Mayes   Southwark Social Services Department
John McLean   National Institute for Social Work
Judith Niechcial   Kingston Social Services Department
Sara Noakes   National Children's Bureau
Pat Osborne   Central Council for Education and Training in Social Work
Elizabeth Parmella   Wirral Social Services Centre
Caroline Pickering   Kirklees Personal Services

Rachel Pierce   Education Consultant
Patricia Pilling   Staffordshire Social Services Department
Anthony Roberts   Bradford Community College
Stephen Smith   Warwickshire Social Services Department
Daphne Statham   National Institute for Social Work
Jennifer Stone   Kent Social Services Department
Ros Taylor   Gloucestershire Social Services Department
Simon Thompson   Wiltshire Social Services Department
Julie Toner   Sheffield Family and Community Services
John Triseliotis   University of Edinburgh

Colin Vyvyan   Social Services Inspectorate, Wales
George Waterman   St.Bart's School of Nursing
Jenny Weinstein   Central Council for Education and Training in Social Work
Robin Wheeler   Gloucestershire Social Services Department
Louise Winterbottom   Student